BASS RECORDED VERSIONS

25 ESSENTIAL ROCK BASS CLASSICS

ISBN 0-7935-8280-6

HAL•LEONARD®
CORPORATION

7777 W. BLUEMOUND RD. P.O. BOX 13819 MILWAUKEE, WI 53213

Visit Hal Leonard Online at
www.halleonard.com

CONTENTS

4	Another One Bites the Dust	Queen
8	Badge	Cream
14	Brown Eyed Girl	Van Morrison
21	Calling Dr. Love	Kiss
25	Come Together	The Beatles
29	Crossfire	Stevie Ray Vaughan
35	Crossroads	Cream
45	Detroit Rock City	Kiss
51	Free Ride	Edgar Winter Group
55	Funk #49	James Gang
60	Gimme Three Steps	Lynyrd Skynyrd
66	Hey Joe	Jimi Hendrix
74	Iron Man	Black Sabbath
80	Jessica	The Allman Brothers Band
87	Lay Down Sally	Eric Clapton
99	Low Rider	War
102	Money	Pink Floyd
107	My Generation	The Who
113	Owner of a Lonely Heart	Yes
118	Paperback Writer	The Beatles
122	Peg	Steely Dan
125	Roxanne	The Police
129	Start Me Up	The Rolling Stones
136	Sweet Emotion	Aerosmith
139	You're My Best Friend	Queen
143	BASS NOTATION LEGEND	

Another One Bites the Dust

Words and Music by John Deacon

Chorus
w/ Bass Fig. 2, 3 times

An - oth-er one bites the dust. _ An - oth-er one bites the dust. _ And an -

oth - er one gone, and an - oth - er one gone. An - oth - er one bites the dust, __ yeah.

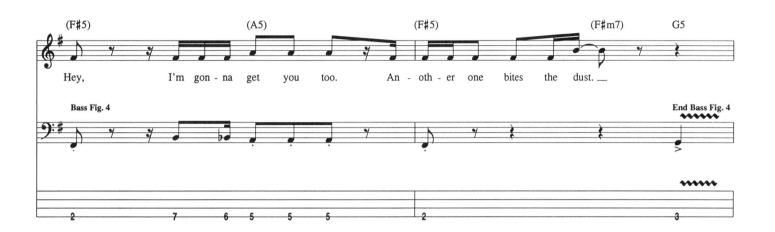

Hey, I'm gon - na get you too. An - oth - er one bites the dust. _

Verse
w/ Bass Fig. 2   w/ Bass Fig. 1   w/ Bass Fig. 2, 2 times

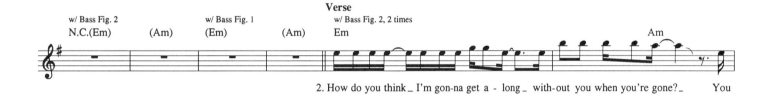

2. How do you think _ I'm gon-na get a - long _ with-out you when you're gone? _ You

w/ Bass Fig. 3

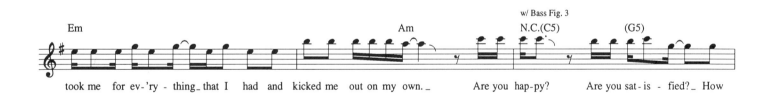

took me for ev - 'ry - thing _ that I had and kicked me out on my own. _ Are you hap-py? Are you sat - is - fied? _ How

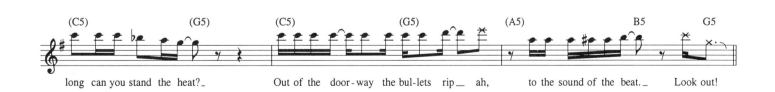

long can you stand the heat? _ Out of the door-way the bul-lets rip _ ah, to the sound of the beat. _ Look out!

Chorus
w/ Bass Fig. 2   w/ Bass Fig. 1

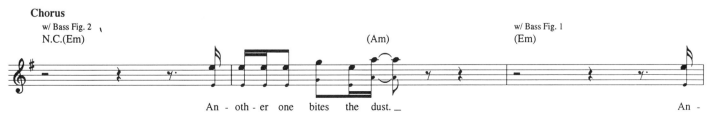

An - oth-er one bites the dust. _ An -

oth-er one bites the dust. __ And an - oth-er one gone, and an-oth-er one gone. An - oth-er one bites the dust. _

Interlude

Hey, I'm gon-na get you too. An-oth-er one bites the dust. _

Bass 1

Bass 1 tacet
N.C.

Hey! Ah, __ take it! Bite the dust! _ Bite the dust _ ah!

Bridge
N.C.

Hey! An - oth-er one bites the dust. _ An - oth-er one bites the dust. _ Ow! _ An-

w/ Bass Fill 1   w/ Bass Fig. 2, 2 times
(Em)

oth-er one bites the dust. _ Hey, hey! _ An - oth-er one bites the dust. _ Hey. _____

Verse
w/ Bass Fig. 1
(Am)   (Em)   (Am)   (Em)

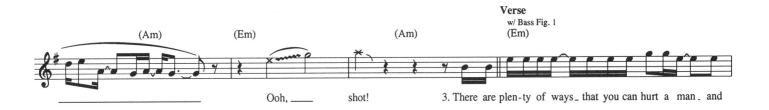

_____ Ooh, ____ shot! 3. There are plen-ty of ways _ that you can hurt a man _ and

Bass Fill 1

bring him to the ground. _ You can beat him, you can cheat him, you can treat him bad, __ and then

leave him when he's down, _ yeah. _ But I'm read-y. Yes, I'm read-y for you. _ I'm stand-in' on my own two feet. _____

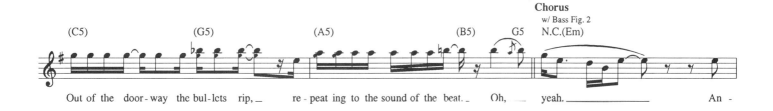

Out of the door-way the bul-lets rip, _ re-peat ing to the sound of the beat. _ Oh, __ yeah. _____ An -

oth-er one bites the dust. _ An-oth-er one bites the dust. _ And an -

oth-er one gone, and an-oth-er one gone. ___ An-oth-er one bites the dust. _

(Yeah.) _____

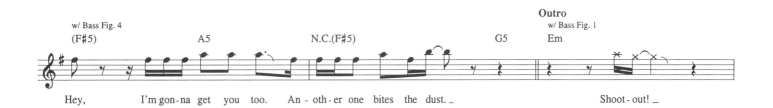

Hey, I'm gon-na get you too. An-oth-er one bites the dust. _ Shoot-out! _

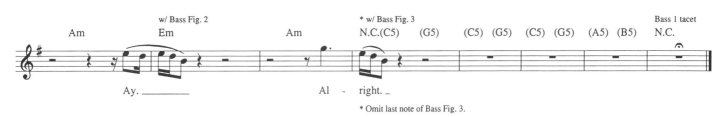

Ay. _____ Al - right. _

* Omit last note of Bass Fig. 3.

Badge

Words and Music by Eric Clapton and George Harrison

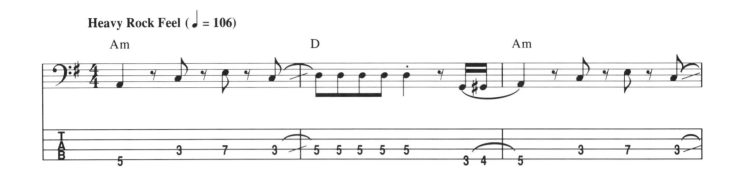

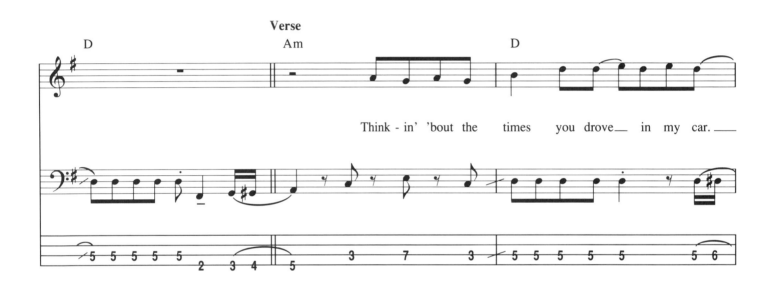

Think - in' 'bout the times you drove— in my car.—

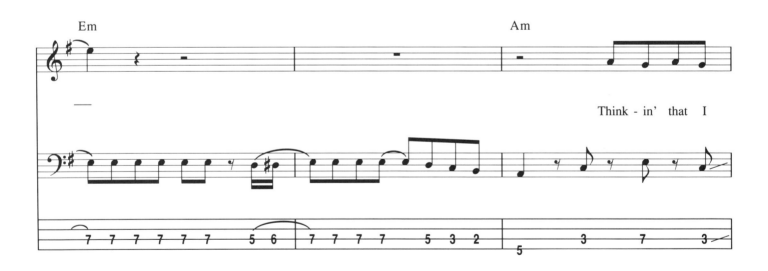

Think - in' that I

I told you 'bout the swans, that they live in the park.

Then I told you 'bout our kid, now he's mar-ried to Ma-

-ble.

Bass is tacet

Bridge

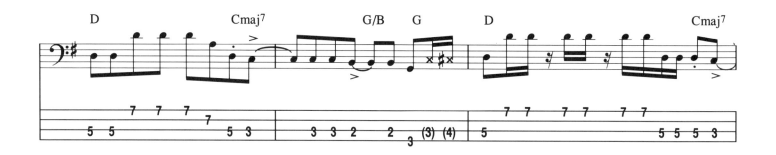

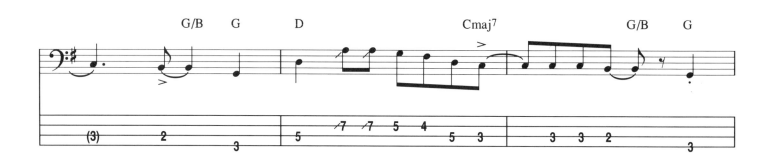

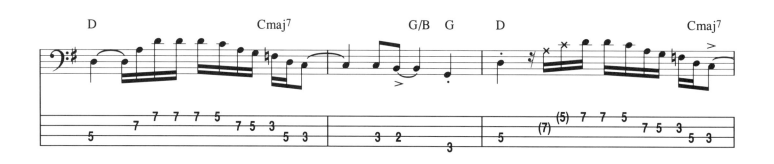

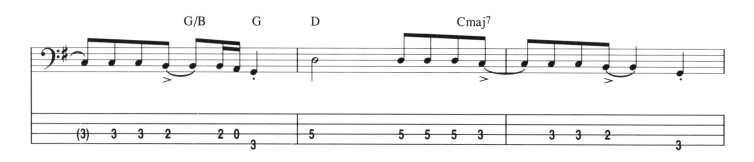

Brown Eyed Girl

Words and Music by Van Morrison

Laugh-ing and a run-ning, hey, — hey, — skip-ping and a jump-ing,

in the mis-ty morn-ing fog — with our, our hearts a thump-in'. And you —

my brown-eyed — girl.

Yeah, you, —— my —— brown-eyed girl. —

la, la, la, la, la, la, la, te, da. La, te, da.

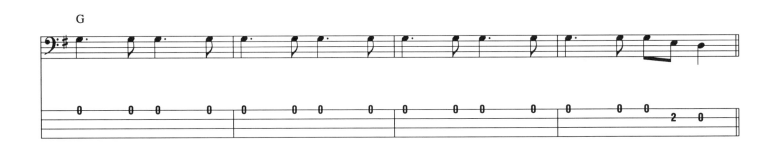

Bass Interlude

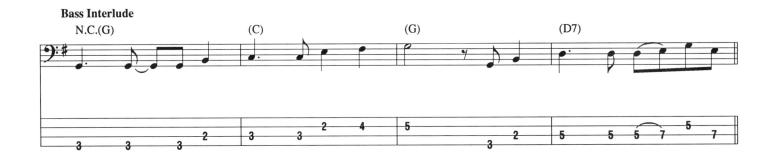

N.C.(G) (C) (G) (D7)

Verse

3. So hard to find ____ my way now ____ that I'm all ____

Calling Dr. Love

Words and Music by Gene Simmons

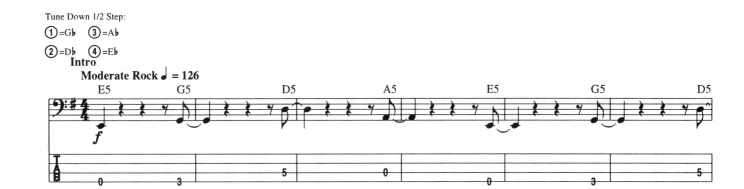

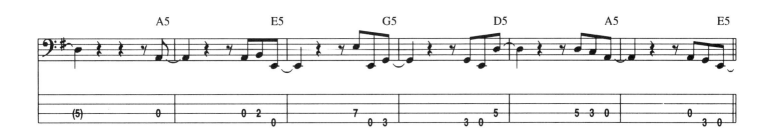

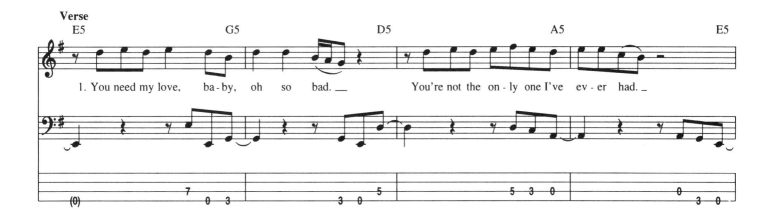

Verse

1. You need my love, ba-by, oh so bad. __ You're not the on-ly one I've ev-er had. __

And if I say I want to set you free, __ don't you know you'll be in mis-er-y. __

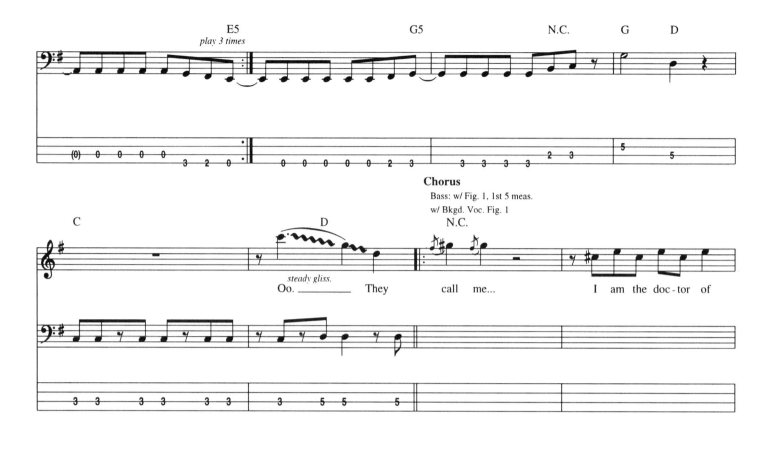

Chorus
Bass: w/ Fig. 1, 1st 5 meas.
w/ Bkgd. Voc. Fig. 1

Oo. _____ They call me... I am the doc-tor of

love. _____ I've got the cure you're think-in' of. _____

Oo. They Yeah. They call me... They call me Doc - tor Love. _

Repeat and Fade
(w/ Lead Voc. ad Lib.)

I've got the cure you're think-in' of. _____ Love. Love.

Come Together

Words and Music by John Lennon and Paul McCartney

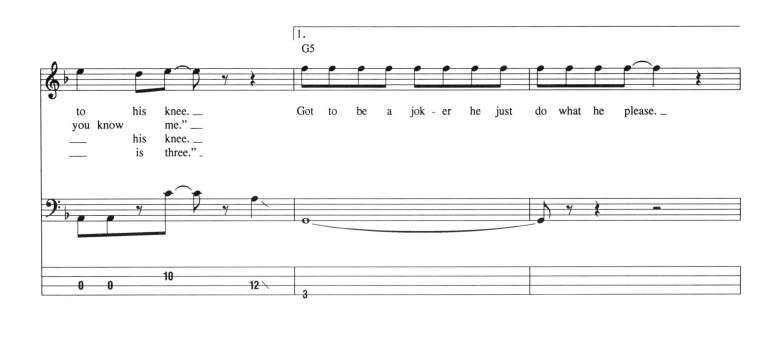

1.
G5

to his knee. __   Got to be a jok - er he just do what he please. __
you know me." __
__ his knee. __
__ is three." -

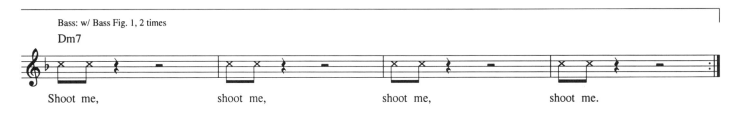

Bass: w/ Bass Fig. 1, 2 times

Dm7

Shoot me,   shoot me,   shoot me,   shoot me.

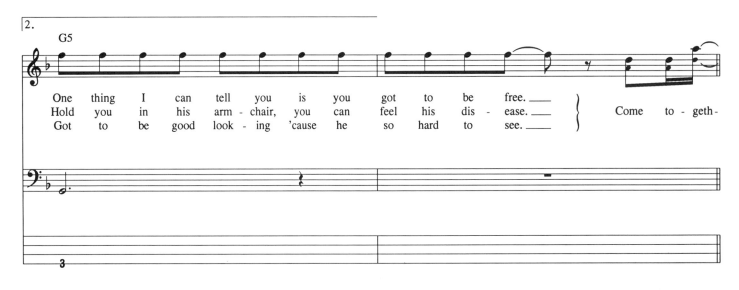

2.
G5

One thing I can tell you is you got to be free. __   Come to - geth-
Hold you in his arm - chair, you can feel his dis - ease. __
Got to be good look - ing 'cause he so hard to see. __

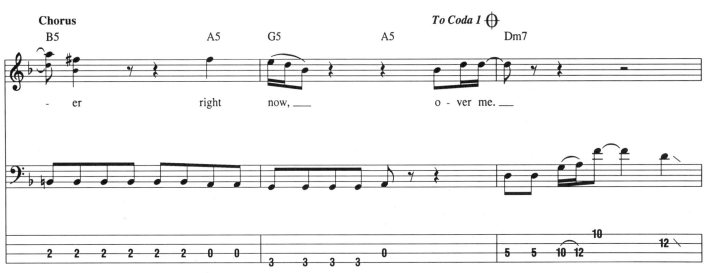

Chorus

To Coda 1 ⊕

B5   A5   G5   A5   Dm7

- er   right now, __   o - ver me. __

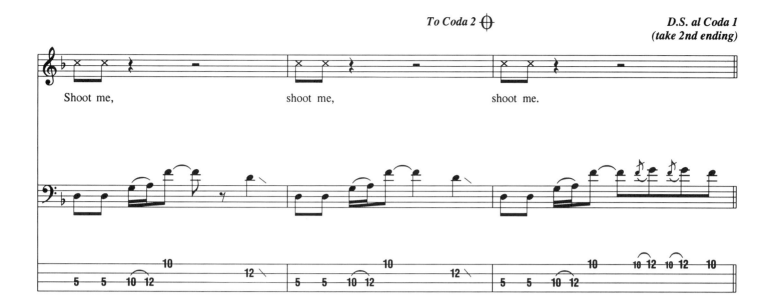

Shoot me,   shoot me,   shoot me.

⊕ *Coda 1*

Keyboard Solo

Dm7   D5

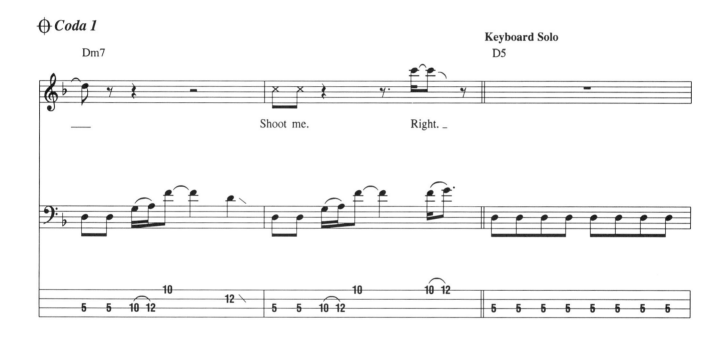

Shoot me.   Right.

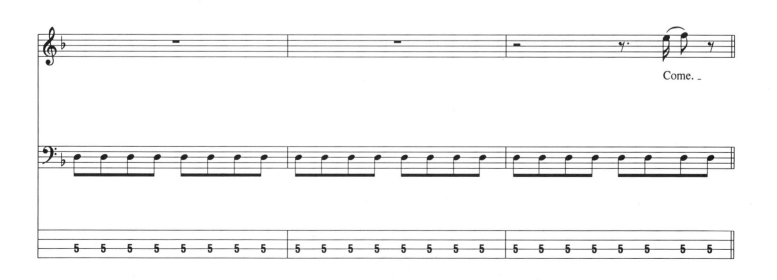

Come.

Guitar Solo

A5

D.S. al Coda 2
(take 2nd ending)

Dm7

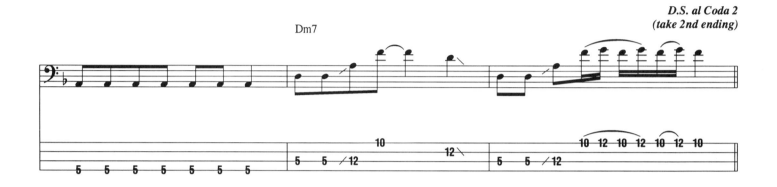

⊕ *Coda 2*

Outro

Shoot me.   Oh.

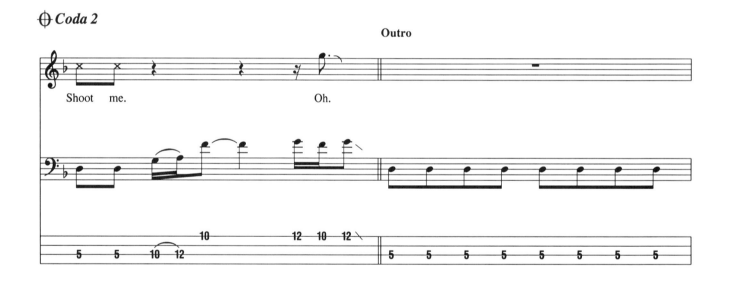

Play 10 Times and Fade

Come to-geth-er,   yeah.

simile on repeats

Crossfire

Written by Bill Carter, Ruth Ellsworth, Chris Layton, Tommy Shannon and Reese Wynans

Tune Down 1/2 Step

①=Gb ②=Db

③=Ab ④=Eb

Moderate "Bluesy" Rock ♩ = 112

Play 3 times

A Introduction

B Verse (E) N.C.

1. Day by day, night af—ter night,__ blind-ed by __ the ne - on lights, __

hur - ry here, hus-tl—in' there,__ no one's got the time to spare.__

Mon-ey's tight, noth-in' free.__ Won't some-bod-y come and res – cue__ me? I am strand-

H Guitar Solo

Verse (G7 / A7)

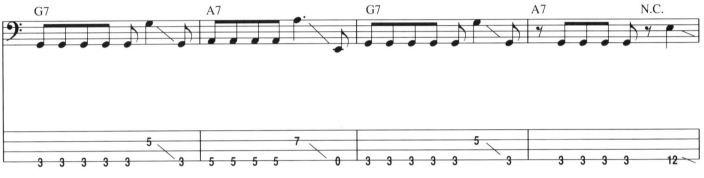

I Verse

3. Save the strong, lose the weak. ___ nev- er turn – ing the oth- er _ cheek. _

Trust no-bod-y, don't be no fool._ What-ev-er hap-pened to the gold-en rule? We got strand-

J **Chorus**
(E7♯9)
N.C.

— ed, _____ caught in ___ the cross - fire. We got strand—

— ed, caught in the cross — fire. We got strand-

K Chorus

- ed,_____ caught in the cross – fire.

Strand - ed, _____ caught in __ the cross - fire. Help me!

L Guitar Solo

(E7)
N.C.

Play 7 times

Crossroads (Cross Road Blues)

Words and Music by Robert Johnson

Blues Rock (♩ = 130)
Instrumental Introduction

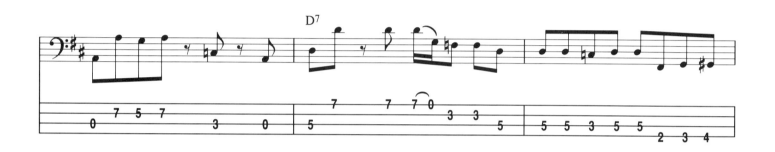

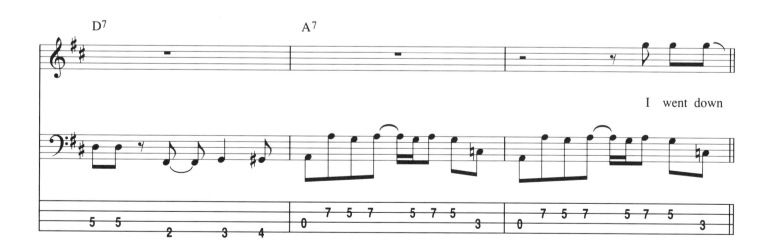

I went down

Verse

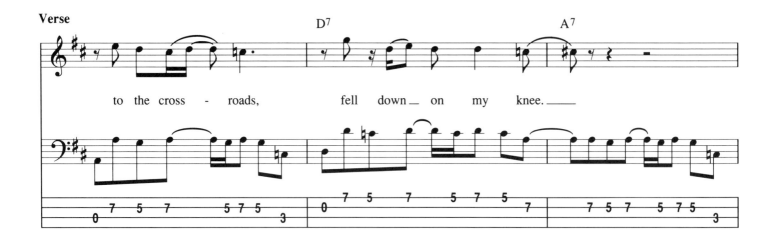

to the cross - roads, fell down__ on my knee.__

Down__ to the cross - roads, fell down__ on my knee.__

__ Ask the Lord a - bove for mer - cy.

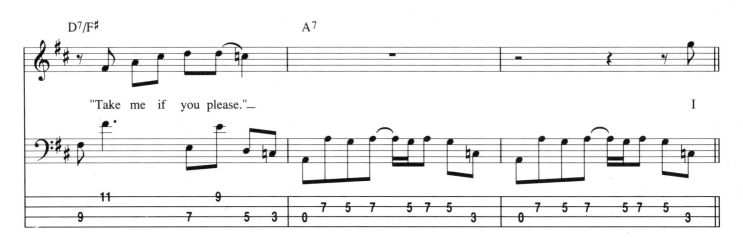

"Take me if you please."__ I

2nd Verse

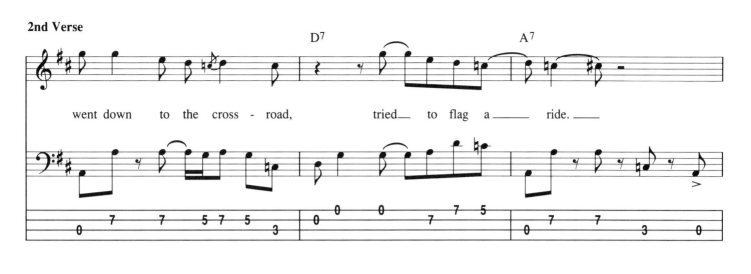

went down to the cross - road, tried__ to flag a _____ ride. ____

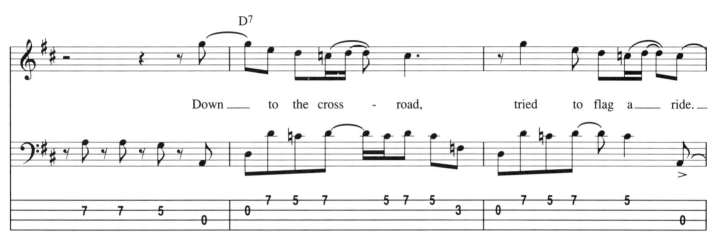

Down _____ to the cross - road, tried to flag a____ ride. __

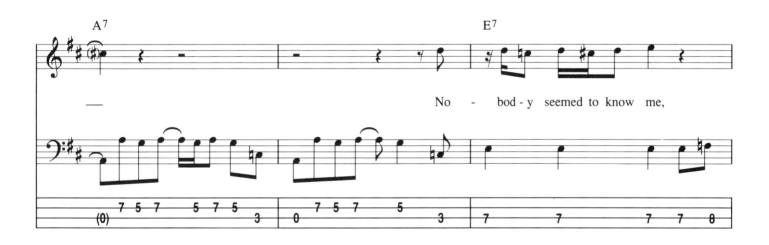

____ No - bod - y seemed to know me,

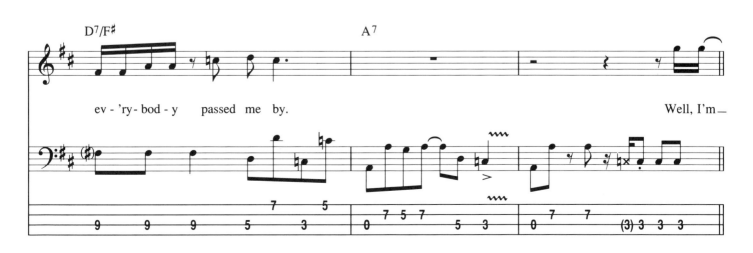

ev - 'ry- bod - y passed me by. Well, I'm__

3rd Verse

goin' down — to Rose - dale, —— take my — rid - er by my side. ——

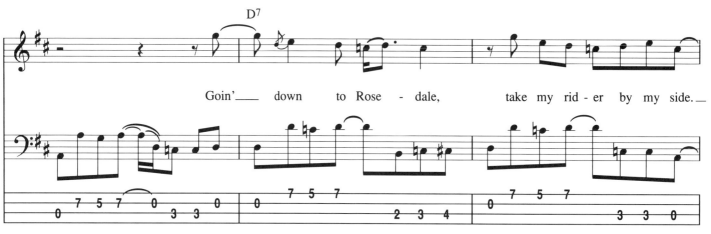

Goin' —— down to Rose - dale, take my rid - er by my side. —

— We can still bar - rel house ba - by, —

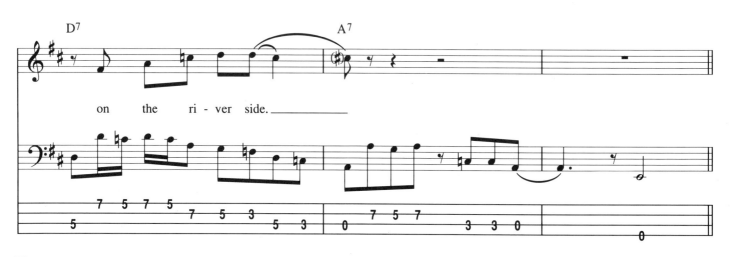

on the ri - ver side. —————

Guitar Solo

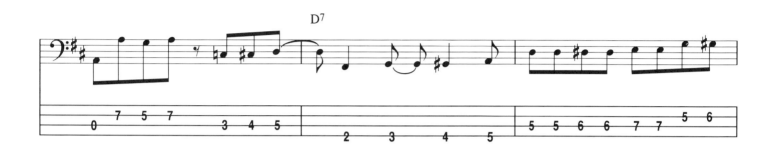

4th Verse

Goin' down __ to Rose - dale, ___ take my __ rid - er by my side. _____

Goin' ___ down to Rose - dale, take my rid - er by my side. __

We can   still   bar - rel house   ba - by, —

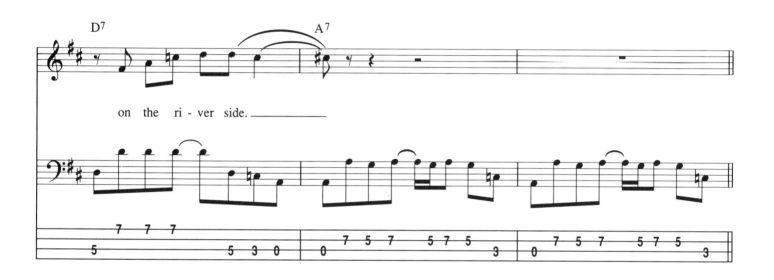

on   the   ri - ver   side. _____

Guitar Solo

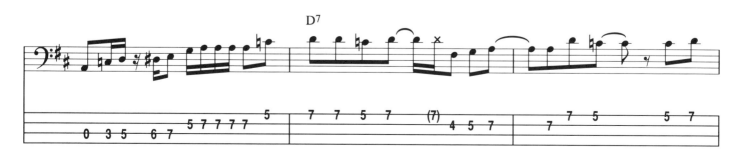

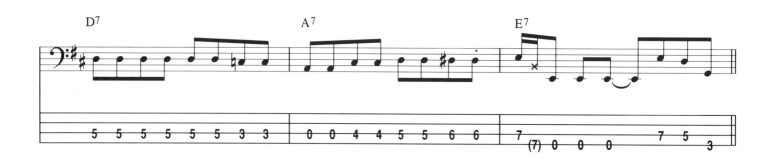

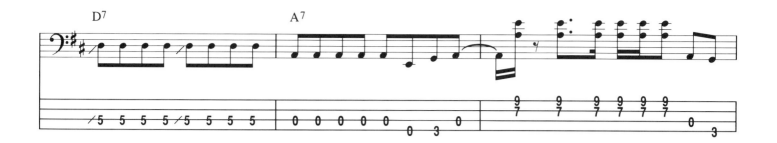

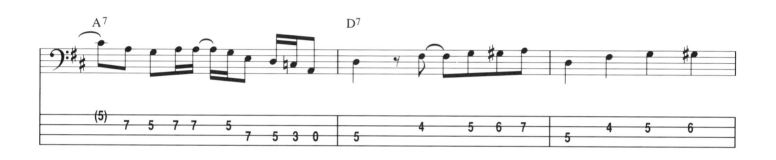

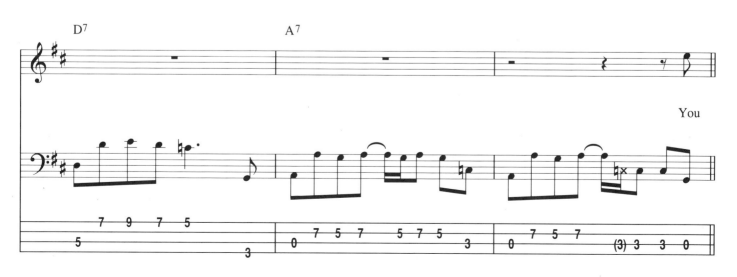

Detroit Rock City

Words and Music by Paul Stanley and Bob Ezrin

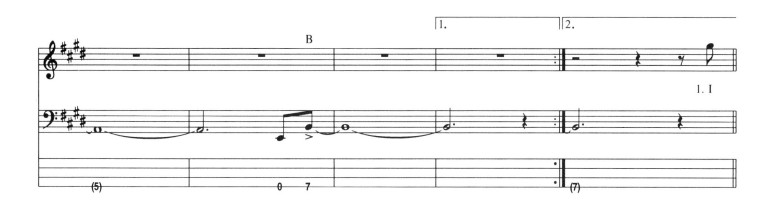

* Chord symbols derived from gtr.

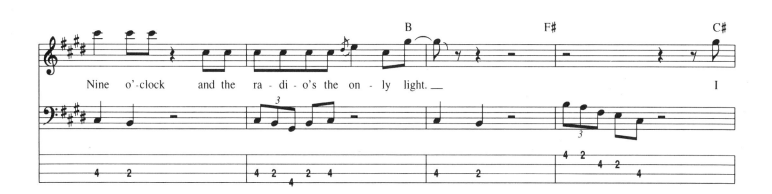

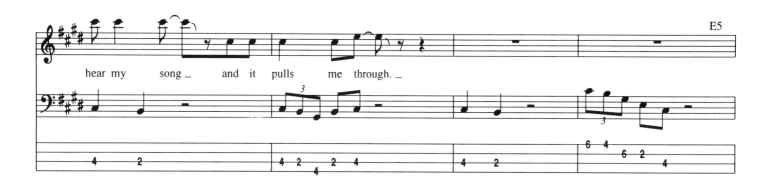

hear my song _ and it pulls me through. _

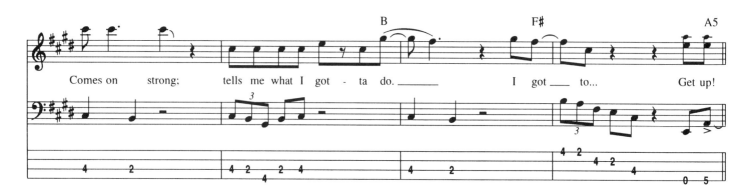

Comes on strong; tells me what I got - ta do. _____ I got ___ to... Get up!

Chorus

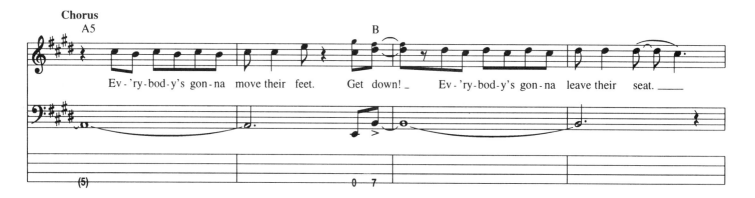

Ev - 'ry-bod-y's gon - na move their feet. Get down! _ Ev - 'ry-bod-y's gon - na leave their seat. _____

You got - ta lose your mind in De - troit Rock Cit - y. Get up!

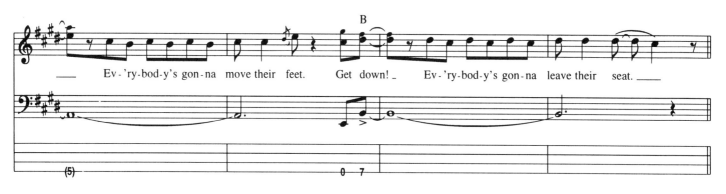

_ Ev - 'ry-bod-y's gon - na move their feet. Get down! _ Ev - 'ry-bod-y's gon - na leave their seat. _____

3. Mov-in' fast, __ do-in' nine - ty - five. __

4. Twelve o' - clock, __ I got - ta rock. __ There's a

Hit top speed, __ but I'm still mov-in' much too slow. _____ I

truck a - head, __ lights star-in' at my eyes. _____

feel so good, I'm so a - live. ___
Oh my God! No time to turn. ___

To Coda ⊕

Hear my song ___ play - in' on the ra - di - o. _____ It goes: ___
got to laugh ___ 'cause I know I'm gon-na die! _____ Why? ___

Get up!. ___

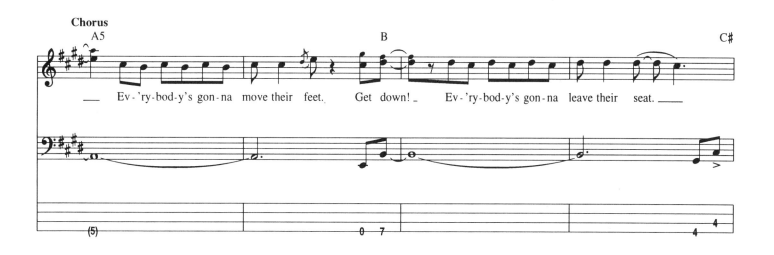

Chorus

___ Ev - 'ry-bod-y's gon - na move their feet. Get down!. ___ Ev - 'ry-bod-y's gon - na leave their seat. ___

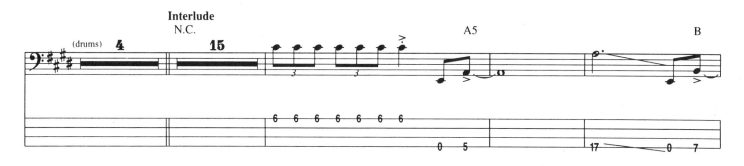

Interlude

(drums)

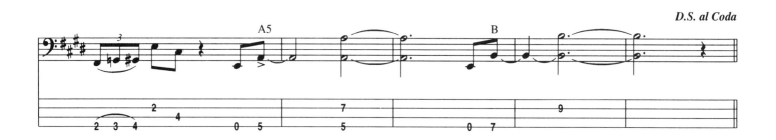

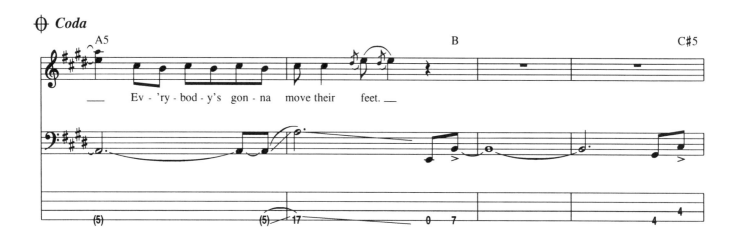

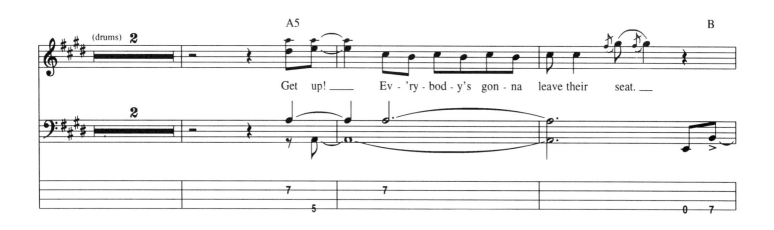

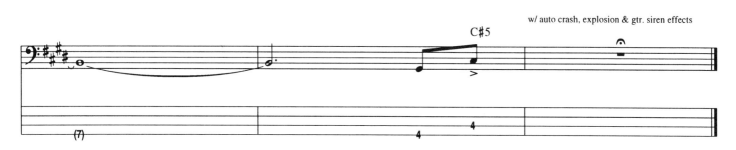

Free Ride

By Dan Hartman

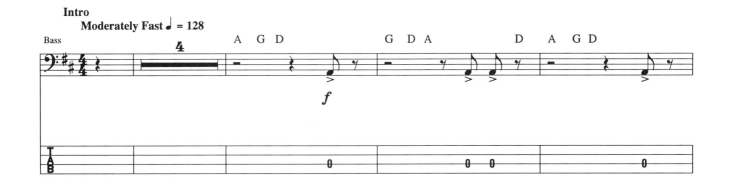

* Doubled an octave below throughout verse.

Funk #49

Words and Music by Joe Walsh, Dale Peters and James Fox

You don't think — that I know your plan; — what you try'n' to hand me?
If you're gon — na act this way, — I think there's trou - ble brew — in'.

Interlude

Percussion Solo

Bass tacet

Guitar Break

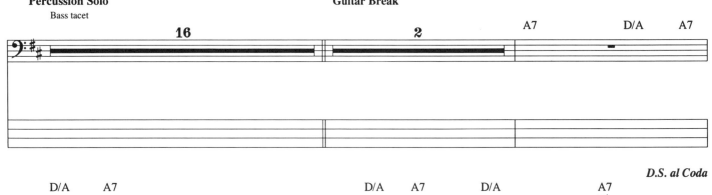

D.S. al Coda

✛ *Coda*

Outro

Gimme Three Steps

Words and Music by Allen Collins and Ronnie Van Zant

MCA Music Publishing

Verse

I was cut-ting the rug __ down at a place called The Jug __ with a

girl named __ Lin - da Lu __ when __ in walked a man __ with a gun in his hand __ and he was

look-ing for you know who. __ He said, "Hey __ there fel-low with the hair col-ored yel - low,

what you try-in' to prove? __ 'Cause that's my wom-an there __ and I'm a man who __ cares __ and this

might be all ___ for you. ___

I was

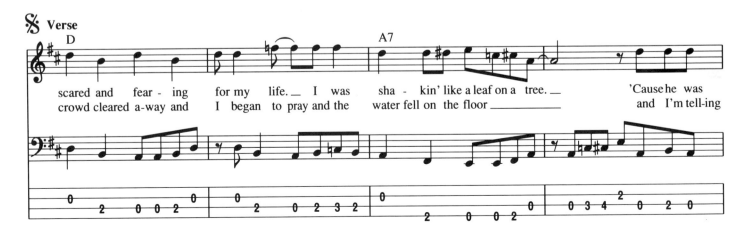

𝄋 Verse

scared and fear - ing   for my life. ___ I was   sha - kin' like a leaf on a tree. ___   'Cause he was
crowd cleared a-way and   I began to pray and the   water fell on the floor _____   and I'm tell-ing

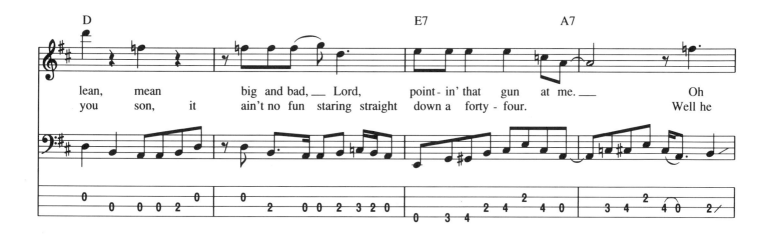

lean, mean big and bad, __ Lord, point-in' that gun at me. __ Oh
you son, it ain't no fun staring straight down a forty - four. Well he

wait a min-ute, mis-ter. I did-n't e-ven kiss her. Don't
turned __ and screamed __ at Lin-da Lu. __ That's the

want no trou-ble with you. _____ And I know
break I was look- ing for _____ and you could

__ you don't owe me but I wish you 'o let __ me ask one fa - vor from you. __
__ hear me scream-ing a mile a - way as I was head-ed out to-ward the door. __

Chorus

last verse

Oh won't you gim - me three steps, gim - me

63

three steps mis - ter. Gim-me three steps to-ward the door. __ Gim-me three steps, gim-me

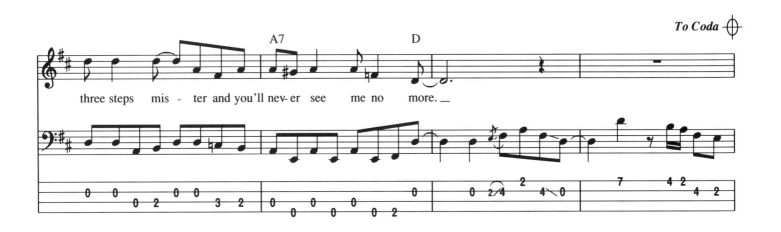

To Coda

three steps mis - ter and you'll nev-er see me no more. __

Solo

Hey Joe

Words and Music by Billy Roberts

Iron Man

Words and Music by Frank Iommi, John Osbourne, William Ward, and Terence Butler

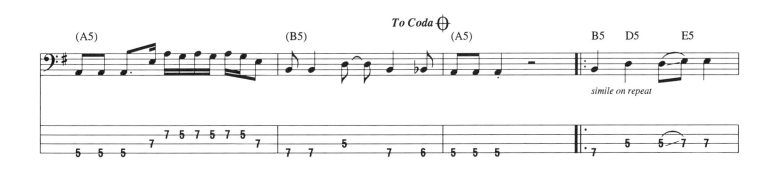

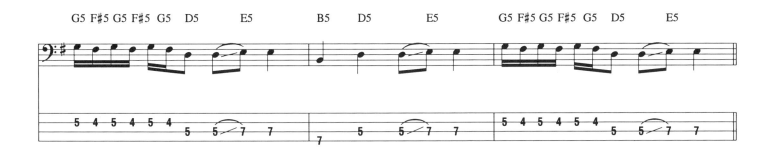

Verse

Bass: w/ Bass Fig. 1, 2 times

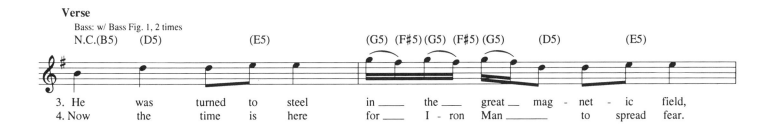

3. He was turned to steel in ___ the ___ great ___ mag - net - ic field,
4. Now the time is here for ___ I - ron Man ___ to spread fear.

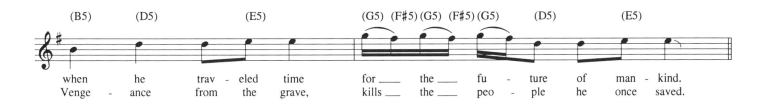

when he trav - eled time for ___ the ___ fu - ture of man - kind.
Venge - ance from the grave, kills ___ the ___ peo - ple he once saved.

Bridge

No-bod-y wants _ him, _ he just stares _ at the world. _
No-bod-y wants _ him, _ they just turn _ their _ heads. _

Bass

Plan - ning his venge - ance _   that he   will _ soon un -
No - bod - y helps _ him, _   now he   has _ his re -

furl. _
venge. _

Interlude

Double-Time ♩ = 164

N.C.(C#m)

Guitar Solo

N.C.(C#m)

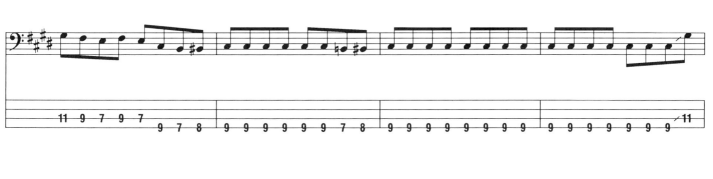

Interlude

End Double-Time ♩ = 76

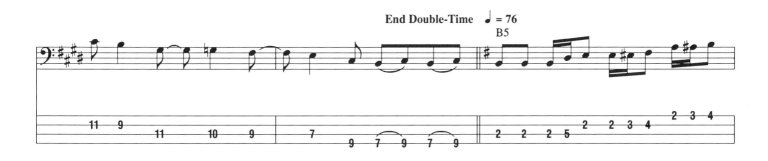

D.S. al Coda
(take 2nd ending)

Coda

Double-Time ♩ = 164

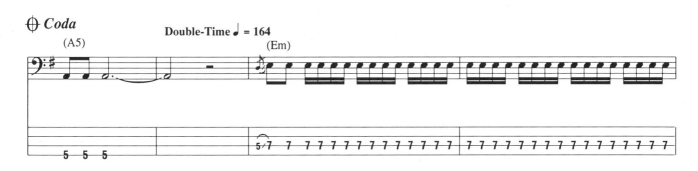

* Chords implied by bass.

Jessica

Words and Music by Dickey Betts

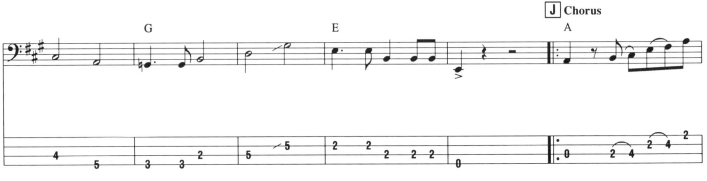

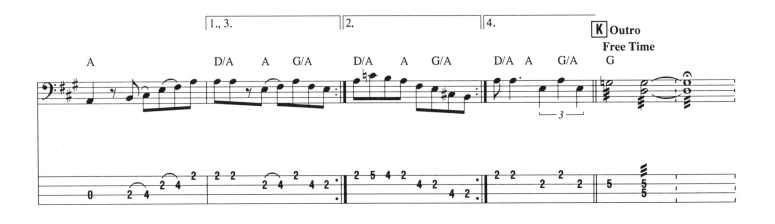

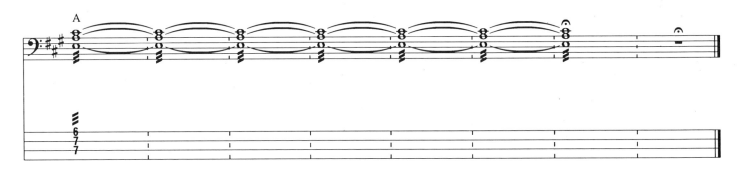

Lay Down Sally

Words and Music by Eric Clapton, Marcy Levy and George Terry

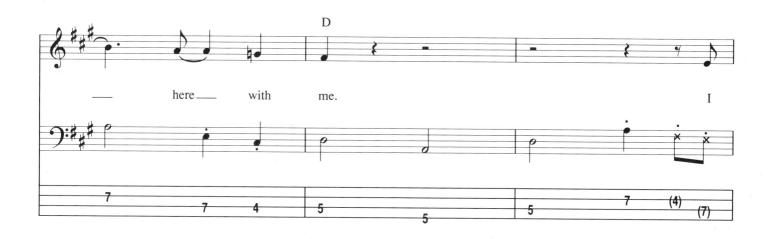

Don't you _ think _ you want ____ some - one __ to talk ____ to?

Lay down Sal - ly, no

need to leave ___ so soon. ____ I've been try - ing all ___

_ night long __ just to talk to you. __

The sun ain't near-ly on ___ the rise, ___ and
we still got ___ the moon ___ and stars ___ a - bove. ___
Un - der - neath ___ the vel - vet skies, ___

I

long to see— the morn - ing light — col - or - ing— your face—

— so dream - i - ly.— So

don't you go— and say— good - bye,— you can lay— your wor -

Lay down Sal - ly, no

need to leave __ so soon. __ I've been try - ing all __

__ night long __ just to talk to you. __

Lay down Sal - ly, and rest here in __ my arms. __

Don't you think___ you want___ some - one___ to talk___

___ to? Lay down Sal -

- ly, no need to leave___ so soon. ___

I've been try - ing all ___ night long ___ just to talk to you. ___

Begin fade

Fade-out

Low Rider

Words and Music by Sylvester Allen, Harold R. Brown, Morris Dickerson, Jerry Goldstein, Leroy Jordan, Lee Oskar, Charles W. Miller and Howard Scott

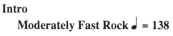

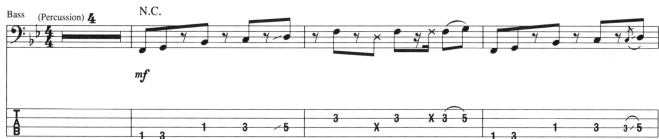

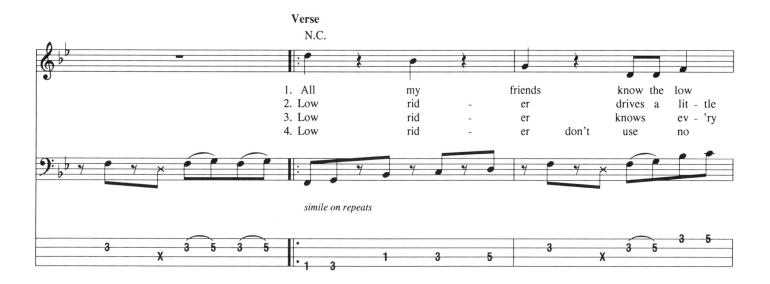

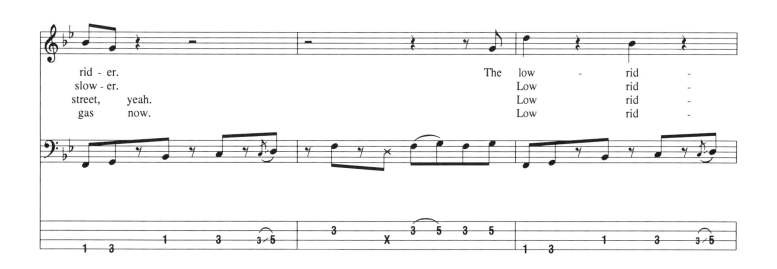

er   is   a   lit - tle   high - er.
er,   he's a   real   go - er.
er,   is   the one to   meet,   yeah.
er   don't drive too   fast.

Chorus

Horns

play 4 times

Outro

Take a lit-tle trip, take a lit-tle trip, take a lit-tle trip and see. _____

Take a lit-tle trip, take a lit-tle trip, take a lit-tle trip with me. _____

Play 3 Times and Fade

Money

Words and Music by Roger Waters

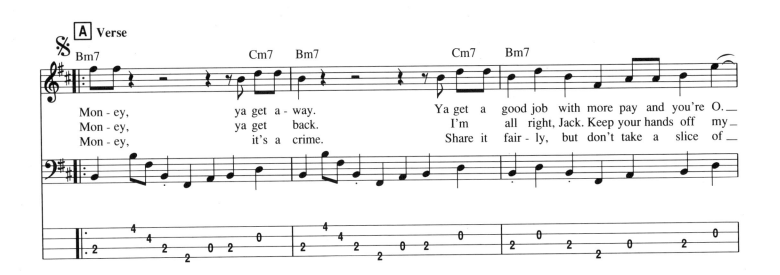

Money, ya get a- way. Ya get a good job with more pay and you're O.
Money, ya get back. I'm all right, Jack. Keep your hands off my
Money, it's a crime. Share it fair - ly, but don't take a slice of

_____ K.
_____ stack.
_____ pie.

Mon - ey,
Mon - ey,
Mon - ey,

it's a gas.
it's a hit.
so they say,

Grab
But don't
is

that cash with both hands and make___ a stash.
give me that do - good-y good bull - shit.
the root of all e - vil to - day.

New car, cav-i- ar, four - star, day-dream.
I'm in the high fi - del - i - ty, first - class trav - 'ling
But if you ask for a rise it's no sur -

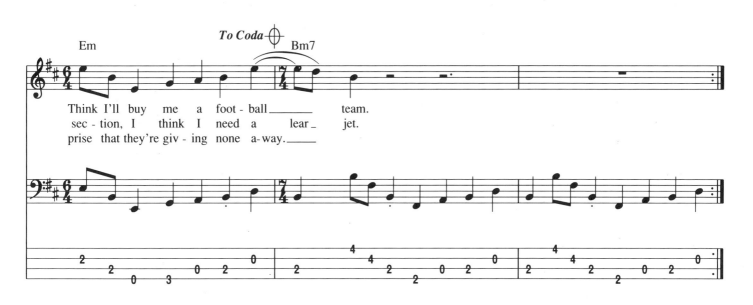

Think I'll buy me a foot - ball _____ team.
sec - tion, I think I need a lear _ jet.
prise that they're giv - ing none a - way. _____

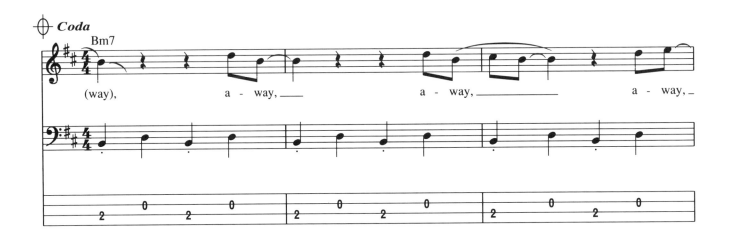

106

My Generation

Words and Music by Peter Townshend

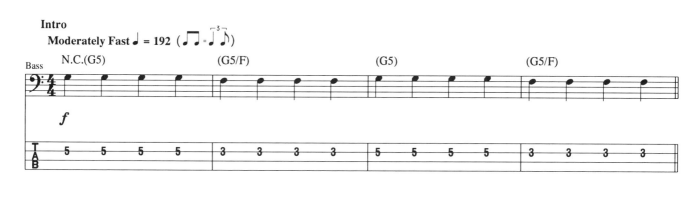

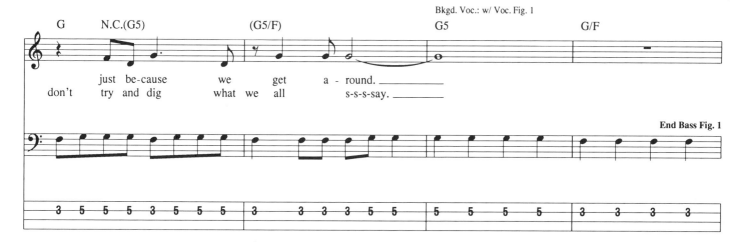

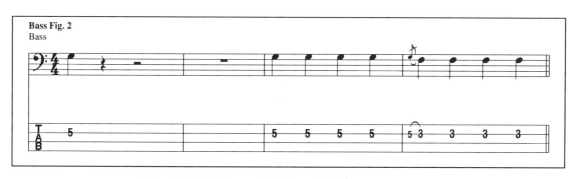

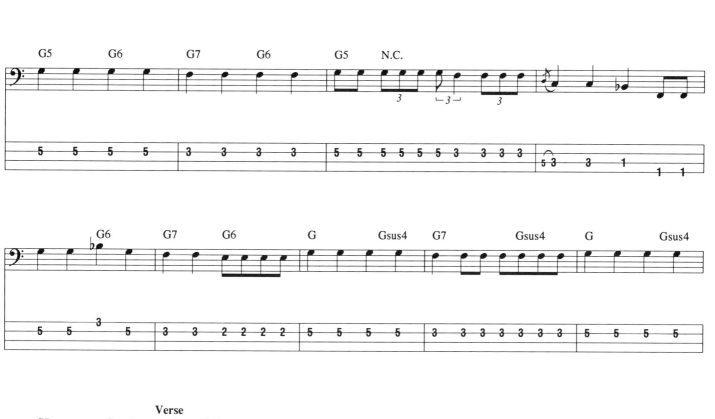

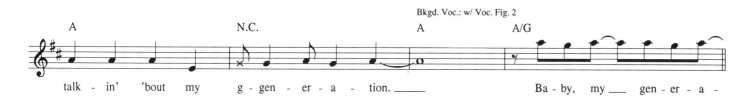

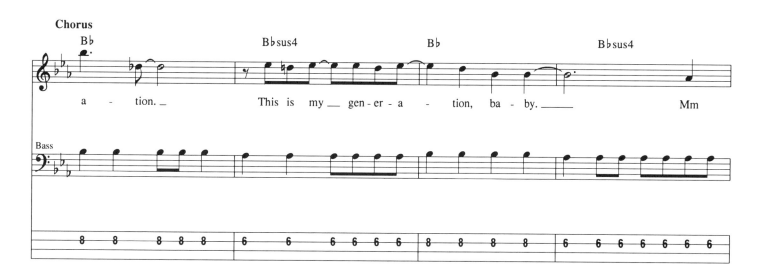

Chorus

Guitar Solo

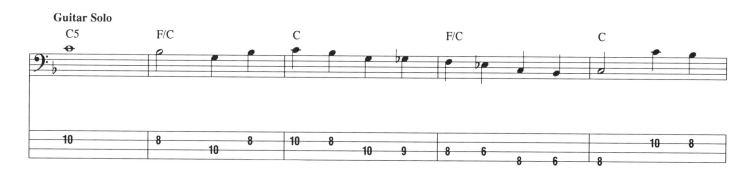

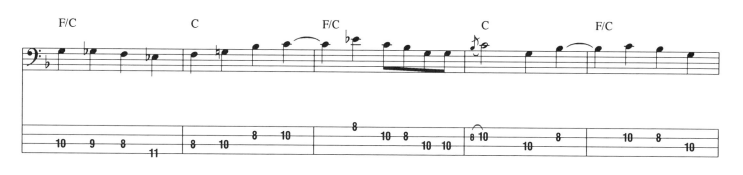

Owner of a Lonely Heart

Words and Music by Trevor Horn, Jon Anderson, Trevor Rabin and Chris Squire

116

Paperback Writer

Words and Music by John Lennon and Paul McCartney

Intro
Moderately Fast Rock ♩ = 166

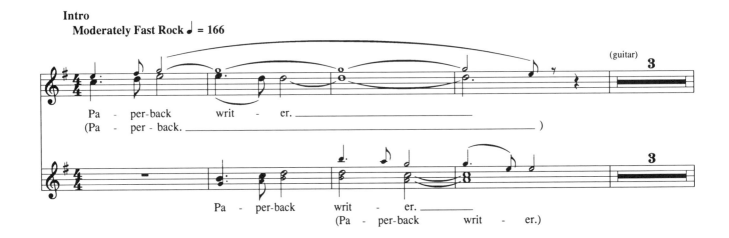

Pa - per-back writ - er. ___
(Pa - per-back. ___)

Pa - per-back writ - er. ___
(Pa - per-back writ - er.)

Verse
G

1. Dear Sir or Ma - dam will you read my book? It took me
3. It's a thou - sand pag - es, give or take a few; ___ I'll be
(Fre - re

* Bkgd. voc. sung 2nd time.

Bass

𝆑
simile on repeat

years to write, ___ will you take a look? It's based on a no - vel by a
writ - ing more ___ in a week or two. I can make it long - er if you
Jac - que. Fre -

writ - er, _____ pa - per - back writ - er. _____

Outro

Bass tacet

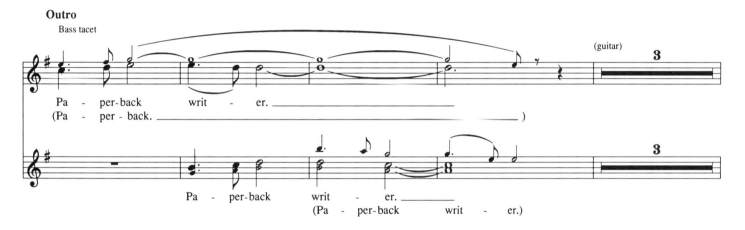

(guitar)

Pa - per - back writ - er. _____
(Pa - per - back. _____)

Pa - per - back writ - er. _____
(Pa - per - back writ - er.)

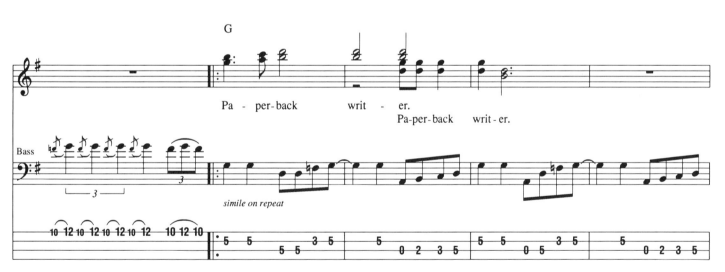

G

Pa - per - back writ - er.
Pa - per - back writ - er.

Bass

simile on repeat

Repeat and Fade

Pa - per - back writ - er.
Pa - per - back writ - er.

Peg

Words and Music by Walter Becker and Donald Fagen

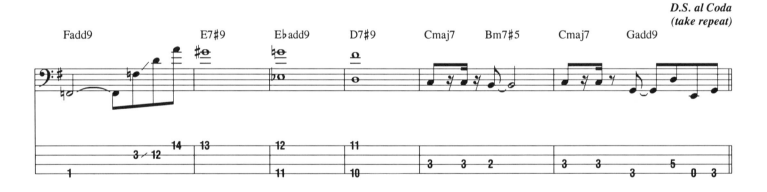

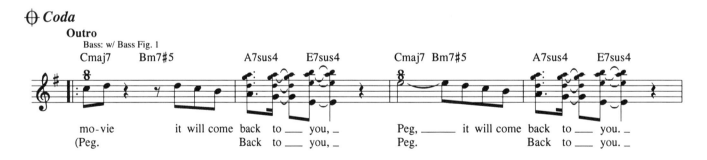

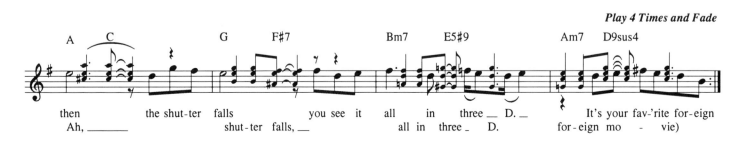

Roxanne

Written and Composed by Sting

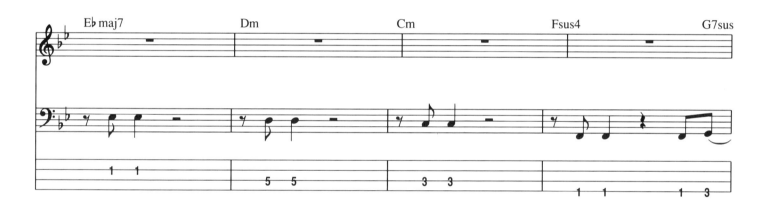

Rox - anne,
loved you since I knew you.
you ___ don't have to ___
I

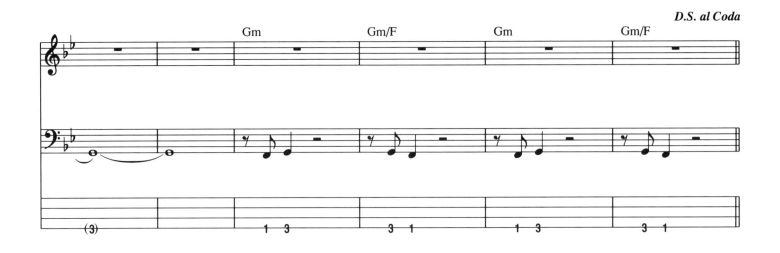

Gm   Gm/F   Gm   Gm/F

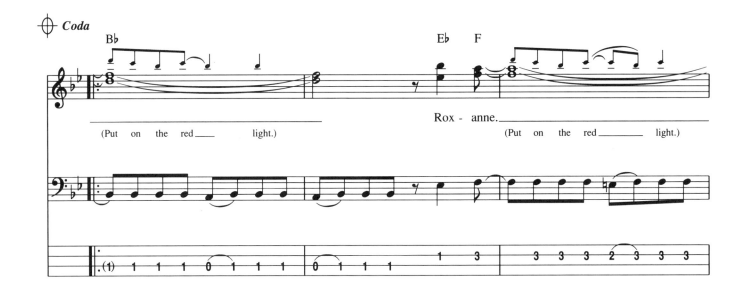

Coda

Bb   Eb   F

(Put on the red ____ light.)   Rox - anne. ____

(Put on the red ____ light.)

Repeat and Fade

F   Gm   Cm   Bb

Rox - anne. ____   Rox - anne. ____

(Put on the red ____ light.)

Start Me Up

Words and Music by Mick Jagger and Keith Richards

Sweet Emotion

Words and Music by Steven Tyler and Tom Hamilton

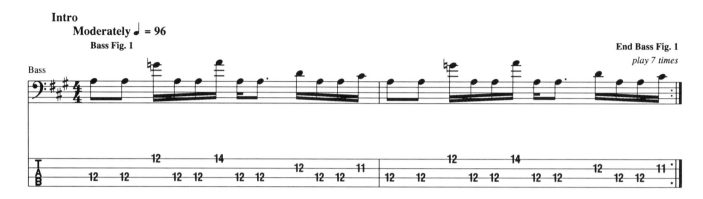

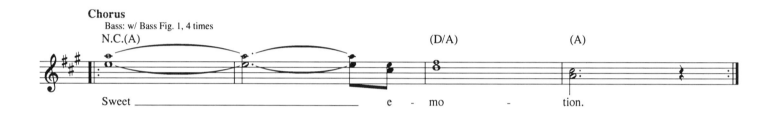

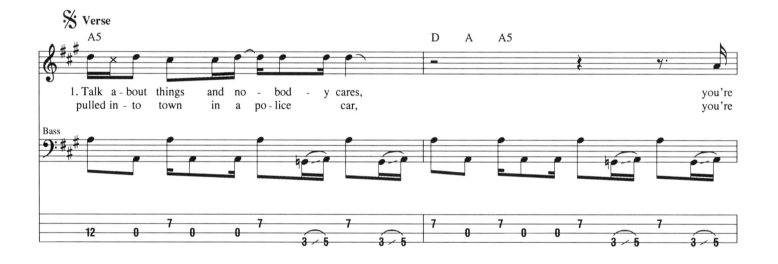

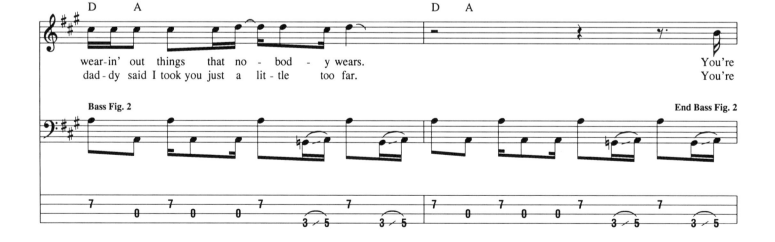

got good news, she's a real ___ good li - ar, 'cause my
talk-in' bout some - thin' you can sure un - der - stand, 'cause a

back - stage boo - gie set yo' pants on fire.
month on the road and I'll be eat - in' from your hand.

Interlude

Bass N.C.

Chorus

Bass: w/ Bass Fig. 1, 4 times, simile

D.S. al Coda

Sweet ___ e - mo - tion tion. 3. I

Coda

Outro

Play 12 Times and Fade

You're My Best Friend

Words and Music by John Deacon

Bass Notation Legend

Bass music can be notated two different ways: on a *musical staff*, and in *tablature*.

THE MUSICAL STAFF shows pitches and rhythms and is divided by bar lines into measures. Pitches are named after the first seven letters of the alphabet.

TABLATURE graphically represents the bass fingerboard. Each horizontal line represents a string, and each number represents a fret.

Notes:

Strings:

3rd string, open   2nd string, 2nd fret   1st & 2nd strings open, played together

HAMMER-ON: Strike the first (lower) note with one finger, then sound the higher note (on the same string) with another finger by fretting it without picking.

PULL-OFF: Place both fingers on the notes to be sounded. Strike the first note and without picking, pull the finger off to sound the second (lower) note.

LEGATO SLIDE: Strike the first note and then slide the same fret-hand finger up or down to the second note. The second note is not struck.

SHIFT SLIDE: Same as legato slide, except the second note is struck.

TRILL: Very rapidly alternate between the notes indicated by continuously hammering on and pulling off.

TREMOLO PICKING: The note is picked as rapidly and continuously as possible.

VIBRATO: The string is vibrated by rapidly bending and releasing the note with the fretting hand.

SHAKE: Using one finger, rapidly alternate between two notes on one string by sliding either a half-step above or below.

NATURAL HARMONIC: Strike the note while the fret hand lightly touches the string directly over the fret indicated.

MUFFLED STRINGS: A percussive sound is produced by laying the fret hand across the string(s) without depressing them and striking them with the pick hand.

BEND: Strike the note and bend up the interval shown.

BEND AND RELEASE: Strike the note and bend up as indicated, then release back to the original note. Only the first note is struck.

RIGHT-HAND TAP: Hammer ("tap") the fret indicated with the "pick-hand" index or middle finger and pull off to the note fretted by the fret hand.

LEFT-HAND TAP: Hammer ("tap") the fret indicated with the "fret-hand" index or middle finger.

SLAP: Strike ("slap") string with right-hand thumb.

POP: Snap ("pop") string with right-hand index or middle finger.

Additional Musical Definitions

(accent) • Accentuate note (play it louder)

(accent) • Accentuate note with great intensity

(staccato) • Play the note short

⊓ • Downstroke

∨ • Upstroke

D.S. al Coda • Go back to the sign (𝄋), then play until the measure marked "***To Coda***," then skip to the section labelled "***Coda***."

D.C. al Fine • Go back to the beginning of the song and play until the measure marked "***Fine***" (end).

Bass Fig. • Label used to recall a recurring pattern.

Fill • Label used to identify a brief pattern which is to be inserted into the arrangement.

tacet • Instrument is silent (drops out).

• Repeat measures between signs.

‖1. ‖2. • When a repeated section has different endings, play the first ending only the first time and the second ending only the second time.

NOTE: Tablature numbers in parentheses mean:
1. The note is being sustained over a system (note in standard notation is tied), or
2. The note is sustained, but a new articulation (such as a hammer-on, pull-off, slide or vibrato begins, or
3. The note is a barely audible "ghost" note (note in standard notation is also in parentheses).

BASS RECORDED VERSIONS

Recorded Versions for Bass Guitar are straight off-the-record transcriptions done expressly for bass guitar. This series features the best in bass licks from the classics to contemporary superstars. Also available are Recorded Versions for Guitar, Easy Recorded Versions and Drum Recorded Versions. Every book includes notes and tab.

Beatles Bass Book
00660103 / $14.95

Best Bass Rock Hits
00694803 / $12.95

Black Sabbath – We Sold Our Soul For Rock 'N' Roll
00660116 / $14.95

The Best Of Eric Clapton
00660187 / $14.95

Stuart Hamm Bass Book
00694823 / $19.95

The Buddy Holly Bass Book
00660132 / $12.95

Best Of Kiss
00690080 / $19.95

Lynyrd Skynyrd Bass Book
00660121 / $14.95

Michael Manring – Thonk
00694924 / $22.95

Alanis Morisette – Jagged Little Pill
00120113 / $14.95

Nirvana Bass Collection
00690066 / $17.95

Pearl Jam – Ten
00694882 / $14.95

Pink Floyd – Dark Side Of The Moon
00660172 / $14.95

Pink Floyd – Early Classics
00660119 / $14.95

The Best Of The Police
00660207 / $14.95

Queen – The Bass Collection
00690065 / $17.95

Rage Against the Machine
00690248 / $14.95

Red Hot Chili Peppers – Blood Sugar Sex Magik
00690064 / $17.95

Red Hot Chili Peppers – One Hot Minute
00690091 / $18.95

Best Of U2
00694783 / $18.95

Stevie Ray Vaughan – In Step
00694777 / $14.95

FOR MORE INFORMATION, SEE YOUR LOCAL MUSIC DEALER,
OR WRITE TO:

HAL•LEONARD® CORPORATION
7777 W. BLUEMOUND RD. P.O. BOX 13819 MILWAUKEE, WI 53213

Prices, contents & availability subject to change without notice.

Stevie Ray Vaughan – Lightnin' Blues 1983-1987
00694778 / $19.95

0498